PRO SPORTS CHAMPIONSHIPS
The Masters

Christine Webster

www.av2books.com

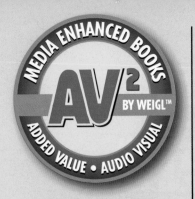

AV[2] provides enriched content that supplements and complements this book. Weigl's AV[2] books strive to create inspired learning and engage young minds in a total learning experience.

Your AV[2] Media Enhanced books come alive with...

Audio
Listen to sections of the book read aloud.

Key Words
Study vocabulary, and complete a matching word activity.

Video
Watch informative video clips.

Quizzes
Test your knowledge.

Embedded Weblinks
Gain additional information for research.

Slide Show
View images and captions, and prepare a presentation.

Try This!
Complete activities and hands-on experiments.

... and much, much more!

Go to **www.av2books.com**, and enter this book's unique code.

BOOK CODE

K 1 3 2 0 9 0

AV[2] **by Weigl** brings you media enhanced books that support active learning.

Published by AV[2] by Weigl
350 5th Avenue, 59th Floor
New York, NY 10118
Website: www.av2books.com   www.weigl.com

Library of Congress Cataloging-in-Publication Data
Webster, Christine.
  The Masters / Christine Webster.
     p. cm. -- (Pro sports championships)
Includes index.
  ISBN 978-1-61913-617-5 (hardcover : alk. paper) -- ISBN 978-1-61913-619-9 (softcover : alk. paper)
1. Masters Golf Tournament--Juvenile literature. 2. Golf--Georgia--Juvenile literature. I. Title.
  GV970.3.M37W43 2013
  796.352'660975864--dc23

                    2012021991

Printed in the United States of America in North Mankato, Minnesota
1 2 3 4 5 6 7 8 9 16 15 14 13 12

062012
WEP170512

Project Coordinator Aaron Carr   Design Terry Paulhus
Every reasonable effort has been made to trace ownership and to obtain permission to reprint copyright material. The publishers would be pleased to have any errors or omissions brought to their attention so that they may be corrected in subsequent printings.

Weigl acknowledges Getty Images as the primary image supplier for this book.

CONTENTS

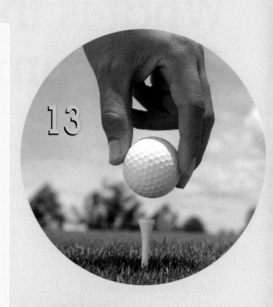

13

21

30

What is the Masters Golf Tournament?

The Masters is a 72-hole golf tournament that takes place over four days in April each year. It is held at the Augusta National Golf Club in Georgia. Since 1940, the Masters has been the first major golf championship of the year. It is one of the four most important golf tournaments in the world.

After a very successful golf career, champion golfer Bobby Jones decided to retire from playing the sport professionally in 1930. Jones and his business partner, Clifford Roberts, wanted to establish a new golf course with a national membership. The men paid $70,000 for a 365-acre (142-hectare) property in Augusta, Georgia. They hired a Scottish architect, Alister Mackenzie, to design the course. Construction began on the site in 1931, and the following year it opened with a limited amount of playing area. The completed course officially opened in 1933. Today, Augusta National Golf Club is one of the best-known golf courses in the world, known for its beauty and challenging play.

When construction was complete, Jones invited a select group of his friends to play on the new course. He challenged them to a friendly tournament, beginning the tradition that led to the Masters Golf Tournament. The tournament has taken place every year since this first event. Thousands flock to Augusta to watch the tournament in person. Millions of other people watch the event on television.

Bubba Watson won the 2012 Masters Tournament.

CHANGES THROUGHOUT THE YEARS

Past	Present
The first golf balls were made from three pieces of leather that were covered in feathers.	Golf balls are made of **synthetic** materials and are dimpled to help them travel farther.
Golf consisted of 13 rules.	There are 34 rules.
Golf club shafts were made out of wood.	Shafts are made from a special type of steel or **graphite**.
Irons, or clubs used for medium distance shots, had smooth faces.	Irons have grooved faces.

The Green Jacket

In 1937, the Augusta National Golf Club designed a members-only coat. The jackets were bought from the Brooks Uniform Company in New York. Members were told to wear the jackets during the Masters Tournament. This was so that other people would be able to easily identify them. At first, the members did not like the idea of wearing the heavy, green coat. A new design, years later, made it more comfortable to wear in the Georgia heat.

The jacket was given to the winner of the Masters Tournament for the first time in 1949. The green jacket had an Augusta National Golf Club logo on the left chest pocket and on each brass button. It is tradition for the previous winner to help the new winner put on the jacket for the first time. The winner keeps the jacket for one year before returning the jacket to the club. Whenever the returning champion visits, the jacket is there for him to wear. In 2011, Phil Mickelson presented the green jacket to Charl Schwartzel.

History of the Masters

Jones challenged his friends to a tournament at the new course. The tournament was so much fun that Jones and Roberts decided to make it an annual event. The first official event took place in March 1934 and was called the Augusta National Invitation Tournament. Horton Smith won the event. Five years later, the name was officially changed to the Masters Golf Tournament.

For three years during World War II, the Masters Tournament was not played. Instead, cattle and turkeys were raised on the grounds. After World War II, the Masters Golf Tournament gained popularity with the help of television coverage. People also enjoyed watching a rising star, Arnold Palmer, play the game. Palmer won the tournament four times between 1958 and 1964. The growing popularity of the Masters Tournament gave it a place as one of the four major professional golfing events.

Bobby Jones and Clifford Roberts died in the 1970s, but they left behind a golf legacy.

Cheered on by his huge fan following, Arnold Palmer won the Masters four times.

During the 1980s, people from countries other than the United States began winning the tournament, including Seve Ballesteros of Spain, who claimed the title twice. However, American golf legend Jack Nicklaus won the tournament six times from 1963 to 1986. He remains the golfer with the most Masters championships.

Though more than 70 years have passed since Jones held the first tournament at Augusta National Golf Course, many of its original traditions have remained in place. For example, only men can play in the event, and the only way for players to take part is to be invited. In most cases, the world's top amateur and professional male golfers are invited to play each year.

In 2002, the National Council of Women's Organizations challenged the Augusta National Club to accept female members. The club refused to change its policy. It decided to remain a male-only club.

Seve Ballesteros of Spain became the first European golfer to win the Masters. He won the tournament twice, in 1980 and 1983.

Features of the Course

The Augusta National Golf Club is considered one of the most beautiful golf courses in the world. It has many notable natural features. For example, President Eisenhower hit his ball into the pine tree at the 17th hole so many times that he asked for the tree to be cut down. Today, it is known as the Eisenhower Tree. Another example is Rae's Creek. The lowest point on the course, the creek was named after the land's former owner, John Rae. It flows along several holes and has bridges crossing it in two places. Augusta National Golf Club also is known for being very neat and tidy. In fact, the green color of napkins handed out with refreshments matches the grass perfectly. This is so that if one of the napkins falls to the ground, it will blend in with the grass.

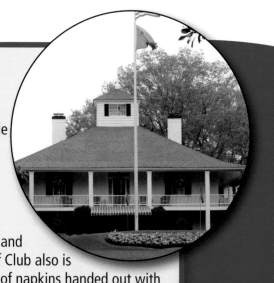

Rules of the Game

Like any sport, golf has rules of the game. There are two main points to know before beginning a game of golf. First, the course must be played as it is when a player arrives. If there has been a hard rain, the ground will be mushy. On a hot summer day, the ground may be hard and dry. Second, the ball must be played from the place where it lands. It cannot be moved to another location. There are special clubs to hit a ball out of a sandy or rough area. If the ball lands in the water, a new ball can be used, but the player will lose a stroke.

1 The Long Game

Players start a round of golf in the tee box, a long way from the small hole they are shooting for. Players use clubs called drivers to try to hit the ball as close to the hole as possible. The score is determined by the number of shots a golfer takes before the ball lands in the hole.

2 Fairways

Once the ball is hit off the tee, it travels along the fairway. The grass is closely cropped along this area that runs between the tee and the green of a golf hole. Players use clubs called irons on the fairway. Irons do not hit the ball as far as drivers, but they offer more accurate aim.

3 Putting Green

Putting is the act of hitting the ball into the hole. To putt, the golfer gently strikes the ball with a club called a putter. Players putt the ball on the putting green. This is a well-groomed grassy area surrounding the hole. The grass here is mowed shorter than any other part of the course.

LEADERS

PRIOR	HOLE	1	2	3	4	5	6	7	8	9	10	11	12	13	14	15	16	17	18
	PAR	4	5	4	3	4	3	4	5	4	4	4	3	5	4	5	3	4	4
	WESTWOOD	0	1	1	0	1	2	3	4	4	3	3	3	4	4				
	MAHAN	0	1	2	2	3	2	1	1	1	1	0							
	CRANE	■	■	■	■	■	■	■	■	■	■	■	■	2	2	2	3		
	JOHNSON Z.	0	1	1	0	0	1	1	1	1	1	1	0	2	2	2	1	2	2
	DUFNER	1	2	2	2	2	2	3	3	3	3	2	2	3	2	3			
	MOLINARI F.	0	1	1	1	1	1	1	1	1	1	1	0	1	1	2	3	3	3
	LAWRIE	0	0	0	0	0	0	1	1	1	1	1	1	1	3	3	4	3	
	WATSON B.	0	0	1	1	1	2	2	2	3	3	2	2	3					
	OOSTHUIZEN	0	0	0	0	0	0	1	0	1	1	0	1	0	1	2	2	3	4
	JIMENEZ	0	1	1	1	0	0	0	0	1	1	1	1	1	2	2	2	3	3

THRU 16

SENDEN	1
BYRD	0
CASEY	3

Weather WARNING

4 Scoring

In a golf game, the person with the lowest score is the winner. Each time a golfer hits the ball, it counts as one stroke. At the end of each hole, the number of strokes the golfer used to sink the ball are recorded. At the end of the game, the total is tallied. This is the golfer's score. Par refers to the number of strokes it should take a golfer to complete the hole. If a hole is par four, it should take four strokes to sink the ball.

5 Etiquette

Etiquette is one of the most important parts of the game of golf. Players are expected to behave in a certain way during a game. For example, if a golfer makes a hole, or divot, in the ground when hitting the ball, that person should repair the grass for the next player. Noise should be kept to a minimum on the course. Golf requires concentration, and loud sounds, talking, and sudden movements can distract players. Golf carts should be driven along paths so as not to damage the course. The player with the best score from the previous hole gets to tee off first at the next hole.

Making the Call

Unlike most sports, golf does not require an official to make calls throughout the game. However, during a golf tournament, a referee usually determines if the rules of the game are being followed. The referee decides if any rules have been broken, and if so, what sort of action to take. An observer is a person who has been appointed to assist a referee.

QUIET Please
HSBC

The Golf Course

Golf courses usually are found on a large piece of land that is about 6,000 to 7,000 yards (5,500 to 6,400 meters) long from the first tee to the last hole. The land is divided into 18 sections, also called holes, that vary from about 100 to 600 yards (90 to 550 m) in length. Each hole has a starting point, called a tee. The land around the tee is level and higher than the rest of the land in the area.

The fairway is a long stretch of land, about 30 to 100 yards (about 27 to 90 m) wide. Here, the grass is cut very short to give a good playing surface. On each side of the fairway is an area called the rough. The rough is not well kept, and there are natural obstacles, such as tall grass, bushes, trees, sand, or marsh, to challenge the golfer. Sometimes, humanmade obstacles are placed on the course. These are called bunkers or traps. They can be hollows in the ground filled with sand or similar material, or they can be mounds, ditches, or ponds.

The Augusta National Golf Course is 7,435 yards (6,799 m) in length.

At the farthest end of the fairway is the putting green. It has closely cropped grass surrounding a hole in the ground. A plastic or metal cup is placed inside the hole, which is about 4.25 inches (10.8 centimeters) in diameter and about 4 inches (10 cm) deep. A flag marks the location of the hole so that golfers know where to aim when they hit the ball off the tee. Each hole is given a number from 1 to 18. A full-sized golf course has 18 holes, though smaller ones may only have nine.

Playing the Game

There are two basic kinds of golf games. They are called match play and stroke play. In match play, the winner is the person who scores the lowest on the most holes. Overall, this person's score may be higher than another player's. In stroke play, the winner is the player who uses the least number of strokes in the entire game. The Masters Tournament uses stroke play rules.

Augusta National Golf Course

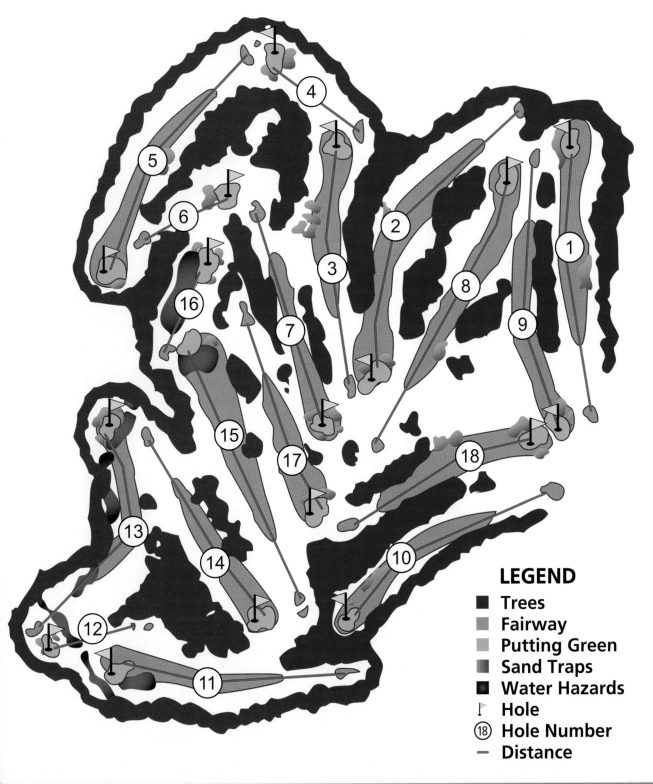

LEGEND
- ■ Trees
- ■ Fairway
- ■ Putting Green
- ■ Sand Traps
- ■ Water Hazards
- ⌐ Hole
- ⑱ Hole Number
- — Distance

Golf Equipment

Sun visor

Glove

Shoes

The main pieces of equipment for a golfer are clubs and a ball. There are three main types of clubs—woods, irons, and putters. Woods and irons come in many shapes and sizes that are used in different situations. Most players carry their clubs and other gear in an equipment bag. They can carry up to 14 clubs during a game.

Woods are used when a player needs to shoot the ball a long distance. Most often, these shots are taken from the tee or a part of the fairway that is a long distance from the putting green.

Irons are used to make precise shots from the fairway. Players use irons called wedges to hit their ball out of traps or the rough when they are near the green. Putters are used when the ball has a short distance to travel to reach the hole.

Golf tees are another important piece of golf equipment. The golf ball is balanced on a tee before players take their first shot on any hole. Usually, tees are made from wood or plastic. They look similar to a nail, with a cup-shaped head for the ball to rest on.

Clubs

Clothing is important in a golf game. Most courses require golfers to dress according to a dress code. Often, players are not allowed to wear jeans, T-shirts, or shorts. Most golfers wear a collared shirt and dress pants.

Special shoes with spikes on the soles are worn to give the golfer a good grip on the grass. Many golfers also wear a glove on one hand to help them grip the club and prevent **blistering**.

Equipment bag

Tee

Golf Balls

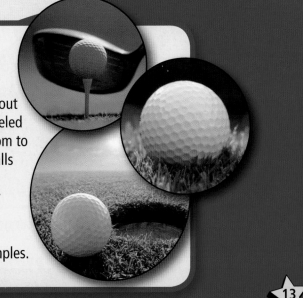

Golf balls are at least 1.68 inches (42.67 millimeters) in diameter and weigh up to 1.62 ounces (45.93 grams). About 100 years ago, it became known that scratched balls traveled farther than smooth balls. This is where the idea came from to put dents, or dimples, on the surface of golf balls. Golf balls today have 330 to 500 dimples. They help the ball move more easily through the air. As a result, players use fewer strokes to sink their ball into the hole. During a game, players may request a ball with a different number of dimples. The best golf balls have between 380 to 432 dimples.

Qualifying to Play

It can take years for a player to qualify to receive an invitation to the Masters. After playing as amateur golfers in various championships, the best players go on to play the sport professionally. Once they have played in and won major tournaments, such as the British Open, the PGA Championship, the U.S. Open, The Players Championship, or the U.S. Amateur Championship, they gain recognition as serious competitors. The Masters Committee reviews the winners of these events to determine who should be invited to play at the Augusta course in April.

There are many factors involved in being able to play in the Masters Golf Tournament. There are 19 ways to qualify for an invitation to the event. Each year, players who meet certain criteria receive an automatic invitation. For example, the top 50 players in the world rankings are all invited. In some cases, the Masters Committee will invite other players that do not qualify officially. Typically, this is done for international players.

Keegan Bradley won the 2011 PGA Championship at the Atlanta Athletic Club in Johns Creek, Georgia.

Rory McIlroy won the 2011 U.S. Open at Congressional Country Club in Bethesda, Maryland.

The Masters has the smallest group of players out of all the major golf championships. Only about 90 players are invited to compete in this tournament. In most tournaments, golfers play in groups of four. However, during the Masters, golfers play in groups of three for the first 36 holes, or the first two days of the tournament. After this, some players are cut from the competition. Players that are not within 44 places of the lead or are more than 10 strokes behind the 36-hole score set by the leader are eliminated from the rest of the tournament.

Once a player has won at the Masters Tournament, he has a lifetime invitation to the event. However, using this invitation is often discouraged. In 2002, the Augusta National Golf Club decided it would be best for players not to play in the event once they reach a certain age.

Tickets for the Masters are sold by application only. Applicants who receive tickets are selected randomly.

19 Ways to Qualify

There are 19 ways for a golfer to qualify to earn a spot to play in the Masters Golf Tournament. One way is to be one of the 50 leaders the week prior to the event, as posted by the Official World Golf Ranking. Another way is to be the current U.S. Amateur champion.

Where They Play

Prior to the tournament, golfers play a practice round at the Augusta National Golf Club.

Unlike other major golf championships, the Masters is held in the same location each year. The Augusta National Golf Club is one of the most **exclusive** golf clubs in the world. Bobby Jones, Clifford Roberts, and Alister MacKenzie worked on the course with Scotland as their inspiration.

The Augusta National Golf Club is known for its beautiful landscaping. Natural flowers, trees, and shrubs are found all over the course. To showcase this feature, in 1940, the date for the tournament was changed from March to the first full week in April. By this time each year, the flowers and shrubs at the course are in full bloom. Each hole on the course is named after a tree or shrub found nearby.

Jim McKay has been Phil Mickelson's caddie in the Masters since 1993. A caddie may help the golfer determine where and how hard to putt the ball.

The greens at the Augusta National Golf Club were originally made from **Bermuda grass**. They were reconstructed in 1981, and **bent grass** replaced the Bermuda grass. Deep green in color, bent grass is thick and low-growing, with a smooth surface.

The Augusta National Golf Club is an exclusive club. It has only about 300 members. Like the tournament, the only way to become a member is by invitation. There are no female members. However, women can play on the course if they are a guest of a member.

For members who want to stay on site, the Crow's Nest is a living space for up to five people. It is one room with partitions to divide it into three spaces, each with a bed. A full bathroom, sitting area, television, and telephone are also found here.

Hundreds of citizens of Augusta leave their homes during the golf tournament. They offer their fully furnished homes to short-term renters during April.

Masters Golf Tournament Winners 2001–2012

YEAR	PLAYER	FINAL	ROUND 1	ROUND 2	ROUND 3	ROUND 4	STROKES	EARNINGS
2012	Bubba Watson	-10	69	71	70	68	278	$1,440,000
2011	Charl Schwartzel	-14	69	71	68	66	274	$1,440,000
2010	Phil Mickelson	-16	67	71	67	67	272	$1,350,000
2009	Angel Cabrera	-12	68	68	68	69	276	$1,350,000
2008	Trevor Immelman	-8	68	68	69	75	280	$1,350,000
2007	Zach Johnson	+1	71	73	76	69	289	$1,305,000
2006	Phil Mickelson	-7	70	72	70	69	281	$1,260,000
2005	Tiger Woods	-12	74	66	65	71	276	$1,260,000
2004	Phil Mickelson	-9	72	69	69	69	279	$1,170,000
2003	Mike Weir	-7	70	68	75	68	281	$1,080,000
2002	Tiger Woods	-12	70	69	66	71	276	$1,008,000
2001	Tiger Woods	-16	70	66	68	68	272	$1,008,000

Mapping the Major Tournaments

U.S. Open

1. 2012 – Olympic Club, San Francisco, California
2. 2011 – Congressional Country Club, Bethesda, Maryland
3. 2010 – Pebble Beach Golf Links, Pebble Beach, California
4. 2009 – Bethpage State Park, Farmingdale, New York
5. 2008 – Torrey Pines Golf Course, La Jolla, California
6. 2007 – Oakmont Country Club, Oakmont, Pennsylvania

PGA

1. 2012 – Kiawah Island Golf Resort, Kiawah Island, South Carolina
2. 2011 – Atlanta Athletic Club, Johns Creek, Georgia
3. 2010 – Whistling Straits, Kohler, Wisconsin
4. 2009 – Hazeltine National Golf Club, Chaska, Minnesota
5. 2008 – Oakland Hills Country Club, Bloomfield Hills, Michigan
6. 2007 – Southern Hills Country Club, Tulsa, Oklahoma

The Masters Golf Tournament is one of four major golf tournaments worldwide. The three other tournaments are the U.S. Open, the British Open, and the PGA Championship. Golfers are only considered among golf's greatest players when they have won one of these major tournaments. When a player wins all four tournaments, they are said to have won the Grand Slam of golf. Only one player has ever won all four majors in the same year. This was done by Bobby Jones in 1930.

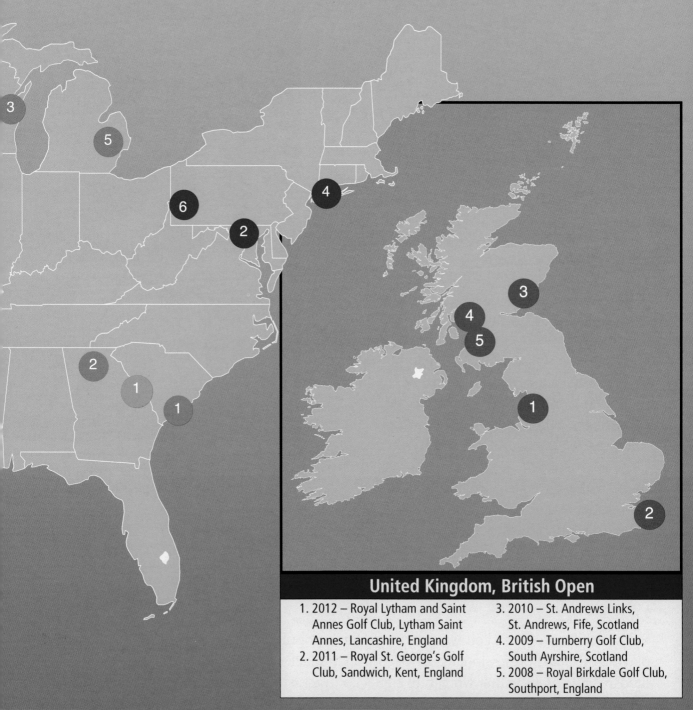

LEGEND

- British Open
- U.S. Open
- The Masters
- PGA

Scale 621 Miles
0   1,000 Kilometers

United Kingdom, British Open

1. 2012 – Royal Lytham and Saint Annes Golf Club, Lytham Saint Annes, Lancashire, England
2. 2011 – Royal St. George's Golf Club, Sandwich, Kent, England
3. 2010 – St. Andrews Links, St. Andrews, Fife, Scotland
4. 2009 – Turnberry Golf Club, South Ayrshire, Scotland
5. 2008 – Royal Birkdale Golf Club, Southport, England

Women and Golf

Although women are not able to play in the Masters Tournament, there are many organizations and tournaments for female golfers. Records show that women have been playing golf since the mid-1500s. In 1867, the first women's golf club, the Ladies' Golf Club, was formed in St Andrews, Scotland. At the time, there were no women playing golf professionally.

Until recently, men and women played golf on different courses. Women's courses were much shorter than men's courses. Today, women often play on the same courses as men, but from tees closer to the hole.

In 1894, the Ladies Golf Union of Great Britain decided to have the first British Ladies Golf Championship. Only amateur golfers played in this tournament. Lady Margaret Scott won the first three championships. The championship was won by British women until 1927. That year, a French woman named Thion de la Chaume took the title. In 1946, the first American woman won the British Women's Open at Gullane in 1947. Her name was Mildred "Babe" Zaharias. The tournament still takes place today, but it is known as the British Ladies Amateur Championship.

Paula Creamer, known as the Pink Panther, is a top-ranked professional golfer on the LPGA tour.

In 1895, the United States Golf Association (USGA) held the first American Women's Amateur Championship. Thirteen women entered. Only one round was played. Lucy Barnes Brown won, with 132 strokes.

By the 1900s, women's golf was becoming quite popular. In the 1920s, women began playing the sport professionally. In 1924, Helen MacDonald signed with Hillerich and Bradsby. She was the first woman to sign a contract with an equipment company.

Ten years later, Helen Hicks was the first woman to promote a manufacturer's products and give golf clinics. She worked with Wilson Sporting Goods.

In the 1930s, there were only four tournaments open to American women. In 1946, the U.S. Women's Open began. Four years later, the Ladies Professional Golf Association (LPGA) was formed. The LPGA hosted 14 events in its first season. Like the PGA tour for men, the LPGA has a year-round golf tour. By 1952, there were 21 LPGA events. Today, the LPGA has about 30 events, and prizes total up to $41 million. Important tournaments for women include the LPGA Championship, the U.S. Women's Open, the Women's British Open, and the Kraft Nabisco Championship. The most important golf events for amateur women are the U.S. Women's Amateur and the British Women's Amateur Championship.

In 1947, Babe Zaharias became a professional golfer.

Michelle Wie

Michelle Wie was born in Honolulu, Hawaii, in 1989. At 10 years of age, she became the youngest player ever to qualify for a U.S. Golf Association amateur championship. She won the Women's Amateur Public Links Championship when she was only 13 years old. This made her the youngest person ever to win an adult USGA championship. Wie turned professional at the age of 15. At 17 years old, Wie earned $20 million in her first year as a professional golfer. She won her first professional tournament in 2009.

Historical Highlights

There have been more than 75 Masters Golf Tournaments since the first event. Over the years, the tournament has had many historical highlights.

One of the most memorable moments in Masters history was when Jack Nicklaus won his sixth title in 1986. After tournament leader Seve Ballesteros hit the ball into the water on the 15th green, Nicklaus saw his chance to take over the lead. Nicklaus shot the ball over the water, and then sunk the putt for an **eagle**. Nicklaus went on to shoot a **birdie** on both the 16th and 17th holes to beat Tom Kite by one shot.

In 1996, Greg Norman seemed the obvious winner, carrying a six-shot lead into the final round. He needed to shoot a par 72 to win the tournament, but he hit **bogeys** on the 9th through 12th holes. In the end, Norman scored 78, losing to Nick Faldo. Norman is one of the world's best-known golfers, but he never has won a Masters.

Jack Nicklaus was the oldest player to win the Masters Golf Tournament, at 46 years old.

Greg Norman was the world's top-ranked golfer for many years, but he never won the Masters.

Tiger Woods and Chris DiMarco battled for the win in 2005. DiMarco led the tournament at the end of the third round, but Tiger jumped ahead by three strokes in the final nine holes. Tiger had one of the most memorable shots in Masters history on the 16th hole, when he chipped the ball in for a birdie. DiMarco attempted to make a chip on the 18th hole, but he was unsuccessful. In the end, Tiger pulled ahead to win the title. It was his first major win in three years.

Most tournament-winning scores are under par. In the case of the Masters, this means the golfer takes 288 strokes or fewer during the entire tournament. Over the history of the Masters, only three players have won with a score above par. They were Sam Snead in 1954, Jack Burke, Jr. in 1956, and Zach Johnson in 2007. They each took 289 strokes.

In 2009, Angel Cabrera of Argentina became the first golfer from South America to win the Masters.

MASTERS GOLF TOURNAMENT RECORDS	
RECORD	**PLAYER**
Most Wins	Jack Nicklaus (6)
Youngest Winner	Tiger Woods (21 years)
Oldest Winner	Jack Nicklaus (46 years)
Most Runner-Up Finishes	Ben Hogan, Jack Nicklaus, Tom Weiskopf (4)
Most Top 5 Finishes	Jack Nicklaus (15)
Most Top 10 Finishes	Jack Nicklaus (22)
Most Top 25 Finishes	Jack Nicklaus (29)
Most Consecutive Years Played	Arnold Palmer (50 years)
Most Total Years Played	Gary Player (52 years)

LEGENDS
and Current Stars

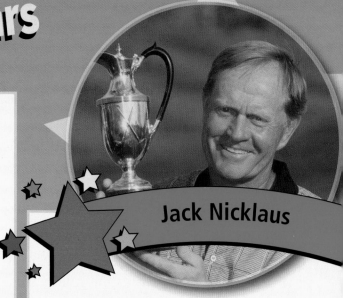

Jack Nicklaus

Arnold Palmer

Arnold Palmer was born in 1929 in Latrobe, Pennsylvania. He is one of the best-known golfers of all time. Palmer began playing golf when he was three years old. He served in the United States Coast Guard from 1950 to 1953. The following year, he won the U.S. Amateur Golf Championship. Palmer decided then to begin his career as a professional golfer. He was the first golfer to win the Masters four times, winning in 1958, 1960, 1962, and 1964. By 1968, Palmer had become the first golfer to earn more than $1 million in tournament prize money. His fans were nicknamed "Arnie's Army."

Jack Nicklaus

Jack Nicklaus was born in Columbus, Ohio, in 1940. Some people believe he is the most talented golfer of the 20th century. Nicklaus began golfing at the age of 10. By the time he was 16, Nicklaus had won his first important tournament—the Ohio Open. Between 1959 and 1986, he set a record for the most victories in golf's Grand Slam tournaments, with 18. From 1959 to 1961, Nicklaus won 29 out of 30 of the amateur tournaments he entered. In 1962, Nicklaus became a professional golfer, and he beat Arnold Palmer that year. This started a rivalry between the two players. Nicklaus won six Masters Golf Tournaments, the most by any player in history. At age 46, he was the oldest winner when he took the title in 1986. Nicklaus is nicknamed the Golden Bear.

Arnold Palmer

Tiger Woods

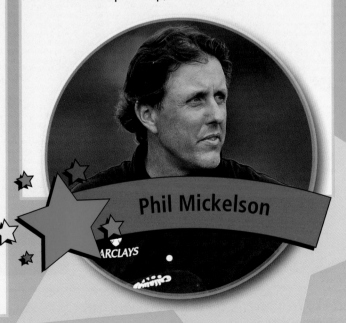

Phil Mickelson

Phil Mickelson was born in 1970 in San Diego, California. He began hitting golf balls at 18 months of age. Mickelson golfs left handed, but he learned the game by mirroring the swing of his father, who is a right-handed golfer.

Mickelson attended Arizona State University. He won three national college championships. In 1990, he became the first left-handed golfer to win the U.S. Amateur championship. In the same year, Mickelson won his first professional tournament while still an amateur. He was only the fourth golfer in history to accomplish this feat.

Mickelson became a professional golfer in 1992. The following year, he won his first tournament as a pro. Mickelson won his first Masters in 2004. He won the Masters again in 2006 and 2010. Mickelson also won another major tournament, the PGA Championship, in 2005.

Tiger Woods

Born in 1975 in Cypress, California, Tiger Woods is one of the greatest golfers of all time. Before the age of 30, he had won each of the game's four major championships at least twice.

Woods began playing golf as soon as he could walk and was featured on many television shows. At 15, he was the youngest player to win the United States Golf Association (USGA) Junior National Championship.

By 1993, Woods had won his third Junior National title in a row. From 1994 to 1996, Woods won three U.S. Amateur Championships. He then turned professional.

In 1997, Woods won his first major victory, the Masters. He set many tournament records. At the age of 21, he was the youngest champion. He also had the lowest score for 72 holes, had the widest margin of victory, and was the first African American golfer to win this event. Woods won the Masters again in 2001, 2002, and 2005.

Phil Mickelson

Famous Firsts

Throughout the history of the Masters Tournament, there have been many special "firsts." From the youngest player to win the title to the first to win more than one in a row, these moments have helped define the event.

In 1966, Jack Nicklaus was the first golfer to win two consecutive tournaments. For this reason, the previous winner could not help him into his own coat. Bob Jones teased that Nicklaus should put it on himself—so he did.

Gary Player from South Africa was the first golfer from overseas to win the Masters. This happened in 1961. Player holds the record for the most appearances in the tournament, at 52. During the 1990s, more golfers from overseas won the Masters than American golfers.

Gary Player won the Masters three times, in 1961, 1974, and 1978. He played his last Masters in 2009.

Mike Weir became the first left-handed golfer in 40 years to win a major golf tournament.

No African American golfers had played in the Masters tournament until Lee Elder in 1975. He received threats from people who believed only golfers of European ancestry should be allowed to take part in this event. Elder paved the way for other African Americans, such as Tiger Woods, to play in the Masters. Tiger is the only African American to ever win the tournament.

In 1997, Tiger Woods became the youngest player ever to win this tournament, at 21 years of age. He has won the tournament a total of four times, and holds the record for the widest winning margin, at 12 strokes, and the lowest winning score, with 270 (-18).

Nick Faldo was the first player from England to win the Masters. He won in 1989, 1990, and 1996.

Special Recognition

There are many reasons to strive for the championship of the Masters. Although popularity, money, and the green jacket are among the most desired, trophies and awards are also prized possessions. The Masters Trophy is awarded to the champion. The trophy was introduced in 1961. It has a model of the Augusta clubhouse mounted on a pedestal. The names of all of the Masters champions are written in the silver bands around the base of the trophy. The main trophy remains at the club, but since 1993, a sterling silver copy has been given to the champion, along with a gold medal and the green jacket. Since 1978, the runners up are given a trophy called the silver salver, and their names are engraved on the championship trophy that is kept at Augusta.

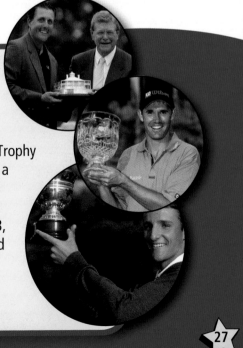

The Rise of the Masters

1931

Construction begins on the Augusta National Golf Course.

1934

Bobby Jones and Clifford Roberts host the first official tournament at Augusta.

1939

The tournament name is officially changed to the Masters Golf Tournament.

1943–1945

The tournament ceases play for three years during World War II. The course is used to raise money for the war effort.

1980

Seve Ballesteros of Spain wins the Masters to become the first golfer from Europe to win the tournament.

1986

Jack Nicklaus wins his sixth championship. This is the record for the most wins.

1997

Tiger Woods becomes the youngest player and first African American to win the Masters.

2003

Mike Weir wins the Masters to become the first Canadian to win a major tournament.

2012

Bubba Watson wins the Masters Golf Tournament.

2002

The National Council of Women's Organizations challenges the no-female members policy of the Augusta National Golf Course.

2005

Tiger Woods beats Chris DiMarco to win his fourth Masters.

QUICK FACTS

- The base of the flagpole in front of the clubhouse is called Founders Circle. Here, there are two plaques engraved with the names of Bob Jones and Clifford Roberts. This is to honor the founding members.

- By 2012, prize money at the Masters Golf Tournament totalled $8 million. The winner earned more than $1.4 million. In the first year, Horton Smith won $1,500 of the total $5,000 in prize money.

- Augusta National Golf Club has a staff of caddies. Female caddies are allowed, even though women are not allowed to be members of the club.

Test Your Knowledge

1 What year was the first Masters Golf Tournament played?

2 Who is the player to win the most titles?

3 Who is the youngest person to win the title?

4 Where is the Masters played each year?

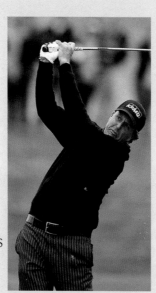

5 Does the Masters Golf Tournament rotate through different courses each year?

6 Besides money, what is the major prize at this tournament?

7 How many ways can a golfer qualify for the Masters?

8 Are women allowed to play at this tournament?

9 Who is the oldest player to win the title?

10 Name the three other major golf tournaments.

ANSWERS: 1) 1934 2) Jack Nicklaus 3) Tiger Woods 4) Augusta, Georgia.
5) No, it is played every year at the Augusta National Golf Club. 6) The Green Jacket,
the Masters Trophy, and a gold medal 7) 19. 8) no, only men 9) Jack Nicklaus, at age 46
10) The U.S. Open, the British Open, and the PGA Championship.

Key Words

bent grass: thick grass with shallow roots that is often found in pastures and lawns

Bermuda grass: grass that grows well in poor soil, spreads easily, and recovers well from damage; native to Europe and Africa

birdie: a score of one stroke under par on a hole

blistering: getting small, pus-filled bubbles on the skin that are caused by rubbing

bogeys: scores of one stroke over par on a hole

eagle: a score of two strokes under par on a hole

etiquette: a code of behavior in a particular place

exclusive: to only admit certain people

graphite: a soft black or gray form of carbon

synthetic: humanmade

Index

Log on to www.av2books.com

AV² by Weigl brings you media enhanced books that support active learning. Go to www.av2books.com, and enter the special code found on page 2 of this book. You will gain access to enriched and enhanced content that supplements and complements this book. Content includes video, audio, web links, quizzes, a slide show, and activities.

Audio
Listen to sections of the book read aloud.

Video
Watch informative video clips.

Embedded Weblinks
Gain additional information for research.

Try This!
Complete activities and hands-on experiments.

WHAT'S ONLINE?

Try This!	Embedded Weblinks	Video	EXTRA FEATURES
Try a golf activity.	Learn more about the Masters.	Watch a video about the Masters.	**Audio** Listen to sections of the book read aloud.
Test your knowledge of golf equipment.	Read about legendary professional golfers through history.	Watch a video about star golfers.	**Key Words** Study vocabulary, and complete a matching word activity.
Label the features of a golf course.	Find out more about golfers who have won the Masters.		**Slide Show** View images and captions, and prepare a presentation.
Complete a timeline activity.			**Quizzes** Test your knowledge.

AV² was built to bridge the gap between print and digital. We encourage you to tell us what you like and what you want to see in the future.

Sign up to be an AV² Ambassador at www.av2books.com/ambassador.